TOTAL KARATE

J. Allen Queen

Sterling Publishing Co., Inc.   New York

To my father, Paul Willis Queen,
a gentle man who demonstrated a "quiet dignity"
and a love for the art of karate.

Edited by Timothy Nolan

Library of Congress Cataloging-in-Publication Data

Queen, J. Allen.
    Total karate / by J. Allen Queen.
        p.   cm.
    Summary: A training guide to karate, detailing the exercises,
skills, and techniques involved in competition stances, self-defense
maneuvers, and other aspects of the sport.
    ISBN 0-8069-6714-5
    1. Karate—Juvenile literature.   [1. Karate.]   I. Title.
GV1114.3.Q45   1990
796.8'153—dc20   89-49313
                                                                    CIP
                                                                    AC

1   3   5   7   9   10   8   6   4   2

Copyright © 1990 by J. Allen Queen
Published by Sterling Publishing Co., Inc.
387 Park Avenue South, New York, N.Y. 10016
Distributed in Canada by Sterling Publishing
% Canadian Manda Group, P.O. Box 920, Station U
Toronto, Ontario, Canada M8Z 5P9
Distributed in Great Britain and Europe by Cassell PLC
Artillery House, Artillery Row, London SW1P 1RT, England
Distributed in Australia by Capricorn Ltd.
P.O. Box 665, Lane Cove, NSW 2066
Manufactured in the United States of America

CONTENTS

ACKNOWLEDGMENTS

I would like to thank the students of the International Children's Karate Association and the Children's Karate Academy of Charlotte, North Carolina, for their assistance in making this book possible.

1
TOTAL KARATE

Huehnergarth

Illus. 1. "Point!" The judge points to you; the crowd screams and claps. You just won the championship in a karate tournament!

Karate was originally designed to be an art form, like dancing. To do karate you combine leg, arm, and foot movements for self-defense, but *you don't actually hit anyone when you practise karate*.

The art of karate developed in the Orient hundreds of years ago. It's origins are unclear; however, it is believed that the first karate techniques were developed by men watching animals fight.

Illus. 2. Such skills as the cat stance are practised by karate students today.

Illus. 3. You would only hit a person if he or she were attacking you or trying to hurt you. From the beginning, you learn to stop your punches and kicks before you touch your opponent or sparring partner.

Illus. 4. Sport karate is perhaps the most popular aspect of karate today.

Sport karate gained popularity with all age groups during the sixties. Today you can enter a karate tournament in every state in the United States and in many countries throughout the world. They are held year-round, mostly on Saturdays. You can enter to win trophies and prizes almost as often as you wish.

When you enter a tournament, you will be able to choose the events you wish to compete in. Usually you can enter two or three events.

Illus. 5. You can do *kata* (ka-TAH), in which you demonstrate before a group of judges a prearranged set of karate moves. In kata you combine karate punches, kicks, and body movements into a graceful demonstration of your karate ability.

Illus. 6. In kata, you have three to five judges; each judge scores each karate player completing a form, or kata, on a score from one to ten, with the highest average score winning. Trophies are given to first through fourth places in each of the age and rank divisions. Judges are always of black belt rank and rate according to your form, speed, and the difficulty of your kata.

Illus. 7. You can also enter the sparring event *kumite* (koo-ME-tay). In kumite, you wear protective equipment and spar an opponent of equal size, age, and rank. Matches are usually two or three minutes long. The fighter who scores the first three points (or who has the most points if less than three) wins the match. In case of a tie, players go into sudden victory with the first score winning.

Illus. 8. In most tournaments there are three judges calling a match—a center judge who serves as the head referee, and two side judges. Two of the three judges must agree for a point to be awarded. Kumite matches continue until there are first- through fourth-place winners.

Illus. 9. You can also enter self-defense events. Self-defense players usually perform in a team or group. Usually three to five participants will enact a scenario of being attacked or robbed. Judges rate the group according to form, originality, and speed.

Illus. 10. As a participant in the sport of karate, especially in kata, a student can show true art form.

To get started in your study of karate, all you will need are a pair of loose pants and a sweat shirt for your workouts at home, but as you continue your study, you may want to buy a karate suit, or a *gi* (GEE). These are required to be worn in tournaments.

Illus. 11 and Illus. 12. Gis come in a variety of sizes, colors, and styles. The traditional suit is white, but the solid black suit has gained popularity in recent years. Some students choose to mix colors, add stripes, or wear a club or school patch on their gi. Inexpensive gis can be purchased at sports stores or ordered from karate magazines.

Illus. 13. You can practise in any large room, garage, or open space. In most karate classes, punching bags, mirrors, weights, and gloves are available for use.

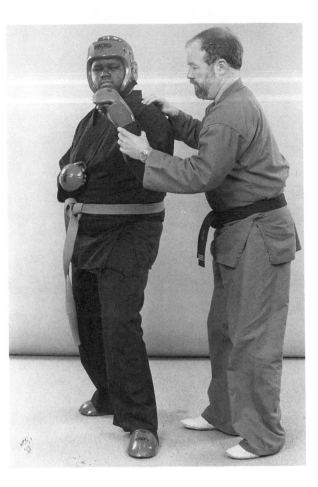

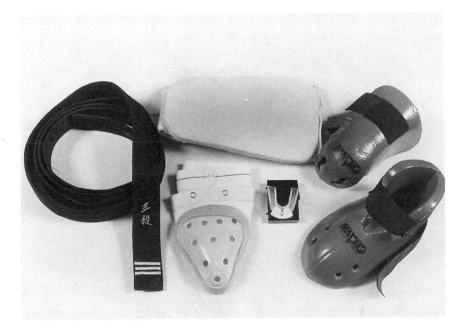

Illus. 14. Purchase your own mouthpiece and do not allow anyone else to use it. The mouthpiece helps to keep you from biting your tongue if you are accidentally hit in the jaw. Hand and feet gloves form to the shape of your hands and feet and give extra protection when you spar with another person. Boys should wear a cup athletic supporter.

Illus. 15. With your suit you will need a belt. There are four major colors of belts that show a person's rank in karate: white for beginners, green for intermediates, brown for advanced levels, and black for experts. Some instructors use additional colors to show ranks between the four major belts.

The karate techniques introduced in this book will take you through the seventh level (yellow belt) and sixth level (orange belt) of study. After six months of continuous practice, you may want to join a karate school which has a special class for children and try out for the fifth level, the green belt.

2
WARM-UP EXERCISES

Huehnergarth

Get into a habit of exercising before karate practice. Your muscles can be easily hurt without proper warm-up exercises, and stretching makes you more flexible and enhances your balance and speed.

Begin these exercises slowly, gradually increasing your movement. Exercise should never be painful. It is a good idea for you to have a checkup by your doctor before beginning any exercise program, especially if you are overweight or if you have a special medical problem.

Do these exercises in order daily, before beginning karate practice. You should also *slowly* do these exercises after your workout as a cool-down activity.

Neck Roll

This exercise loosens your neck and strengthens the muscles. Repeat it five times to each side. Increase with practice.

Illus. 16 (above left). Stand with your feet a shoulder width apart and turn your head to the left.

Illus. 17 (left). Roll your head back.

Illus. 18 (above). Roll your head to the right, then downwards. Return to a straight position.

17

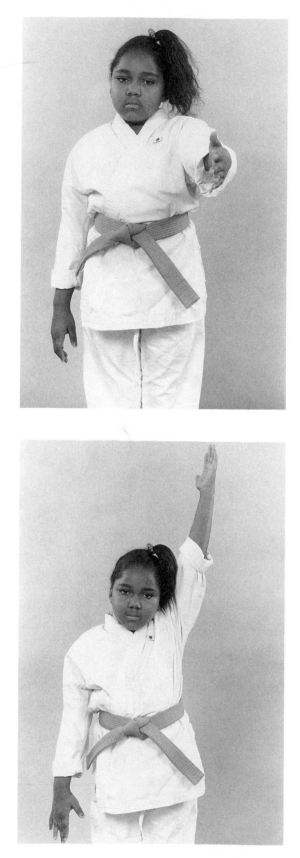

Single-Arm Swing

This exercise loosens your shoulders and arms. Repeat it ten times with each arm.

Illus. 19 (above left). Stand straight with your feet a shoulder width apart and swing your left arm forward.

Illus. 20 (left). Swing your arm upwards.

Illus. 21 (above). Swing it behind you as if you are winding a large clock, and finish with your arm at your side.

Double-Arm Swing

Stand straight with your feet a shoulder width apart.

Illus. 22 (above). Swing both of your arms upwards.

Illus. 23 (above right). Swing them behind you.

Illus. 24 (right). Finish with a swing to your front. Repeat ten times.

Full-Body Bends

Full-body bends will increase your flexibility. Do these *slowly* and don't force too hard. With time and practice you will easily reach the floor.

Illus. 25 (left). Stand straight with your feet a shoulder width apart and your hands touching.

Illus. 26 (below left). Without bending your knees, move downwards and reach as close to the floor as possible. Return to the original position, and repeat five times.

Illus. 27 (below). Bring your feet closer together.

Illus. 28 (below). Do the same move downwards. Repeat five times.

Illus. 29 (right). Finally, place your feet together.

Illus. 30 (below right). Touch the floor without bending your knees.

Cross-Body Bends

Illus. 31. Stand straight and place your feet two shoulder lengths apart. Keep your legs straight. Bend your left arm and touch your right foot. You may not be able to touch your foot at first, but go as far as you can go.

Illus. 32. Come straight up and repeat with the right arm to the left foot. Do twenty of these bends with each arm, alternating left and right.

Leg Stretch

Leg stretches will give you some extra flexibility.

Illus. 33. Sit with your left leg behind you and your right leg straight out in front of you. Bend forward with both hands and try to touch the toes of your right leg.

Illus. 34. Bend as far as you can without hurting yourself. In time you will be able to grab your foot. Repeat ten times with each leg. Try harder with each stretch.

Front-Leg Swing

Leg swings add to balance and flexibility.

Illus. 35. Stand straight with your feet together.

Illus. 36. Swing your right leg up to your waist and lower it. Repeat five times for each leg.

Increase the height of your swing with each repetition. Eventually, you will be able to swing your leg over your head.

Side-Leg Swings

Illus. 37. Stand straight with your feet together. Keep your left leg straight, without bending your knee, and raise it to your belt level.

Repeat ten times; then do the same with your right leg. With each practice session, try to get your leg higher.

Back-Leg Swing

Illus. 38. Start from a standing position and lift your right leg straight up behind you. Be careful and do this slowly. Do not bend your knees. Try to limit bending your body to the front as much as possible.

Toe Grab

Illus. 39. Sit down with your legs straight in front of you. Keep your knees straight.

Illus. 40. Bend over and grab your ankle, foot, or toes. The goal is to reach your toes. Hold the position for a count of five. Repeat ten times.

24

Deep-Leg Bend

These warm up the muscles on the inside of your legs. Move slowly, and go only as far as you can.

Illus. 41. Stand with your left leg pushed in front of you, your right leg straight and to your right side.

Illus. 42. Slowly drop your left knee and begin to lower your weight on that knee. At the same time, lock (do not bend) your right knee and stretch.

Repeat this exercise five times to the left and five times to the right.

Split

Illus. 43. Stand with your feet wide apart and knees bent. Slowly move your right foot forward.

Illus. 44. Move your body over your right leg. Keep your back leg straight.

Illus. 45. Carefully stretch until you can't go any farther. Repeat twice; then go to the right side and repeat twice.

Use your hands for support if needed. Remember not to stretch too hard. Be careful! This exercise will make you more flexible, and give height, power, and speed to your kicks. You will feel some tightness in your inner thighs, but stop if it becomes painful.

Knee Jerks

Illus. 46. Stand with your right leg behind your left leg.

Illus. 47. Jerk your right knee up to your stomach or chest level and return to your original position. Repeat ten times with each knee.

26

3
KARATE SKILLS

Huehnergarth

STANCES

A strong stance is the most important part of karate. Since you are only as strong as your stance, think of it as your solid foundation.

In your stance, keep your shoulders and back straight. Tighten the muscles in your stomach and hips.

Closed Stance

Illus. 48. Use the closed stance with your feet together to begin a kata or do a traditional bow. Place your weight equally on both feet.

Illus. 49. Foot position.

Open Stance

This stance is also known as the ready or set stance. Use it to start and finish most karate exercises.

Illus. 50. Place your feet a shoulder width apart with your weight equally on both feet.

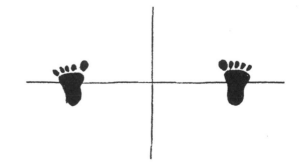

Illus. 51. Foot position.

Front Stance

The front stance lets you move to the front or to the rear. It is one of the strongest and most flexible stances in karate.

Illus. 52. In a left front stance, keep your right leg straight with your knee locked, and place your left leg in front. Bend your left leg at the knee and keep a little more than half your body weight on it. Do the opposite for the right front stance.

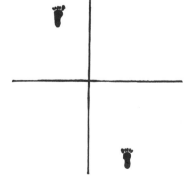

Illus. 53. Foot position.

Back Stance

One of the most used stances is the back stance.

Illus. 54. In the left back stance, put three quarters of your body weight on your left (back) leg. Put the rest of your weight on your right (front) leg. Bend both knees slightly, and form an L-shape with your feet. Do the opposite for the right back stance.

Illus. 55. Foot position.

Cat Stance

The cat stance makes you look like a cat crouching and preparing to strike. With most of your body weight on your back leg, your front leg is free to strike quickly.

Illus. 56. Shift all of your weight to your back leg—your left leg is in a left cat stance. Do the opposite for the right cat stance.

Illus. 57. Foot position.

Horse Stance

The horse stance makes you look like you are riding a horse. In the horse stance, you can use many different types of blocks, strikes, or kicks. It is hard for an opponent to hit you when you are in the horse stance.

Illus. 58. Spread your feet two shoulder widths apart and bend your knees deeply. Place your body weight equally on both legs and feet. Keep your back straight. This stance may be difficult for you to do at first. Practise it until it seems easier.

Illus. 58A. Foot position.

BLOCKS

Punches, strikes, and kicks can be used in offense or defense, but blocks are just for defense. You should know how to deflect an opponent's attack, before learning to attack.

Rising Block

Use the rising block to stop a downward blow to the head.

Illus. 59. Get into an open stance with your left hand across and in front. As you go into a left front stance, bring your left arm across your chest, palm downwards. Your right fist is at your right hip.

Illus. 60. Turn your left arm so that your palm faces upwards and drive it up to meet the strike. Do the opposite for a right rising block.

Outside Middle Block

You can protect your middle and upper body with the outside middle block.

Illus. 61. From a left front stance, push your left hand forward as you pull your right hand back near your head.

Illus. 62. For a right outside middle block, swiftly turn to the right, and drive your right arm completely across your body. At the same time, pull your left arm back to your right hip. Do the opposite for a left outside middle block.

Inside Middle Block

Use the inside middle block to protect your upper body.

Illus. 63. In a left front stance, place your left arm across your chest while placing the right arm on your right hip.

Illus. 64. Like a coiled spring, snap your left arm upwards to block. Do the opposite for a right inside block.

Low Block

Use a low block to block the lower body area.

Illus. 65 (below). Move into a left front stance and place your left arm across your body with your hand near the right side of the head. Keep your right arm resting on the right hip as you move into the block.

Illus. 66 (right). Drive your left hand straight downwards.

Illus. 67 (below right). Keep your left arm out in front and your right hand on your right hip ready to punch.

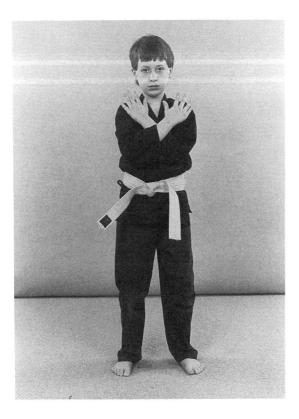

"X" Blocks

Illus. 68 (left). To do an open "X" block, stand with your feet a shoulder width apart. Cross your arms with your hands open (palms in), resting on your chest.

Illus. 69 (below left). Drive your hands downwards while keeping your arms crossed.

Illus. 70 (below). Continue until your arms are fully extended. Practise this move until you can do it quickly.

To do a closed "X" block, make the same moves as for the open "X" block, except close your hands.

Shuto Block

The shuto block, or knife-hand block, can be thrown from a front-stance or back-stance position. Your left hand blocks the attack, while your right hand rests on your chest.

Illus. 71 (below). Pull your left hand back, palm inward.

Illus. 72 (right). Push the hand outward.

Illus. 73 (below right). Turn the knife edge of the hand around to strike.

Hook Block

Use the hook block to grab an opponent.

Illus. 74. From a back-stance or front-stance position, prepare your right hand for a shuto block.

Illus. 75. As you strike out to block, bend your wrist slightly back and grab.

PUNCHES

Making a Fist

Follow these three steps to make a correct karate punch.

Illus. 76 (below). Close your fingers tightly at the second knuckle.

Illus. 77 (right). Roll your fingers into the palm of your hand.

Illus. 78 (below right). Press your thumb over your index and middle fingers.

To remember how to make a fist, use the first word of each step: close, roll, and press.

Front Punch

Illus. 79 (above left). Stand in a ready stance with your right fist held palm upwards at your hip. Hold your left hand in front with your palm held downwards.

Illus. 80 (left). Punch in a straight line, turning your fist until the palm faces downwards.

Illus. 81 (above). At the same time, pull back your left hand and turn it, palm upwards, into a fist. Rest it at your hip.

Illus. 82 (below). Strike with the first two knuckles of your index and middle fingers.

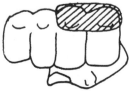

43

Back Fist

Illus. 83 (below). Place your left fist to your chest.

Illus. 84 (right). Like a whip, snap the hand outward in a straight line. When you fully extend the hand, the back of the hand will strike the target.

Illus. 85 (below right). Draw it back in a snapping action to the original position.

44

Reverse Punch

Perhaps the most commonly used punch in kumite today is the reverse punch. It is fast and can be very accurate.

Illus. 86 (left). Stand in either a back, front, or horse stance. Use your left hand to cover your body in case of an attack. Pull your right hand tightly by your side, and turn your body slightly.

Illus. 87 (below left). Push the right hand outward while turning the fist upwards and fully extended.

Illus. 88 (below). Snap the hand back to your chest and move the right hand back into the original position.

Shuto Strike

Illus. 89 (above left). To throw the shuto strike, or knife hand, get into a right back stance and place your right hand behind your head with palm outward.

Illus. 90 (left). As you prepare to strike, turn your upper body slightly as you bring the knife edge of your hand around to strike.

Illus. 91 (above). As you make contact, snap your hand back to the original position. The strength of your shuto depends upon the snapping action of your arm and hand.

Illus. 92. Strike with the shaded area.

Palm-Heel Strike

The palm-heel strike is used to strike the upper face area.

Illus. 93 (above). In any stance, pull your right hand back to your chest with the palm facing away from you.

Illus. 94 (above right). In one quick move, extend the hand outward, striking the target. Keep your left hand pulled back in a position ready to punch.

Illus. 95 (right). Strike with the heel of the palm.

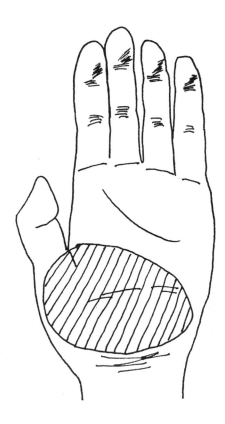

Inside Ridge-Hand Strike

A ridge hand is the reverse of a shuto strike.

Illus. 96 (left). Pull your right hand, palm inward, back to your chest.

Illus. 97 (below left). Throw your hand outward to block a punch.

Illus. 98 (below). Strike with the shaded area.

Outside Ridge-Hand Strike

Illus. 99 (below). Strike with the ridge of the hand, thumb pulled back.

Illus. 100 (right). In a front or ready stance, swing your right arm far behind you and keep the arm straight.

Illus. 101 (below right). In one swift move, swing your arm around with a driving force, finishing the strike with your hand fully extended.

Hammer Strike

Illus. 102 (right). From any stance, pull your left hand back behind your head.

Illus. 103 (left). Strike outward and downwards as though you were striking with a hammer.

Back Elbow

Illus. 104 (left). With the back elbow, push your right arm upside down in front of you. Keep your fist closed.

Illus. 105 (right). Drive your elbow straight behind you. Keep your arm by your side. Use your left hand to cover your right hand for greater striking power.

Side Elbow

Illus. 106 (right). Get into a horse stance. Close your right fist and fold it into your left hand.

Illus. 107 (left). Push your right elbow out to the striking area.

Upward Elbow

Illus. 108 (left). Keep your left hand in front of you for protection. In a horse stance, place your right hand in the punching position.

Illus. 109 (right). With one swift move, jerk the elbow straight up to strike the chin of an opponent. Pull your left hand back to give extra force to the strike. This makes you ready to punch if you need to strike.

Half-Fist

Illus. 110 (below). In a left front stance, position yourself as though you are going to deliver a front punch.

Illus. 111 (right). Deliver the punch, striking *only* with the middle knuckles of each finger.

Illus. 112 (below right). Strike with the shaded area.

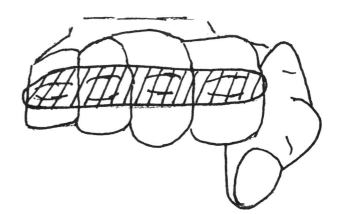

Spear Hand

Like a spear, the spear hand is pointed for striking.

Illus. 113 (right). Get into a punching position and bring your left arm across your body.

Illus. 114 (left). As you punch, open your hand fully and extend your arm. Rest your right arm in your left for support.

KICKS

Your legs are nearly three times as strong as your arms. Therefore, your kicks should be three times as strong as your punches. However, balancing while kicking is difficult. You must learn to shift your weight to one leg when you kick. This will improve with dedicated practice.

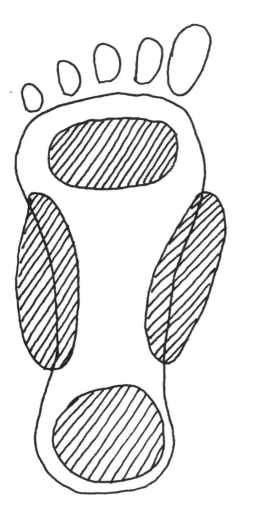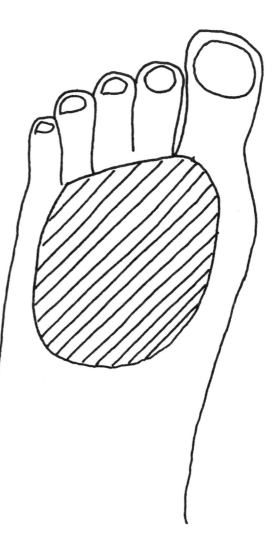

Illus. 115. The foot has six major areas that are used for striking: top, ball, heel, inside edge, outside edge, and the entire bottom.

Front Thrust Kick

Illus. 116 (below). Stand in a left front stance.

Illus. 117 (right). Lift your right leg to your left knee, and pull your body backwards. Drive the kick to the target.

Illus. 118 (below right). Return the kick immediately to the left knee. Place your right leg back into the original position. Do the opposite for a left front thrust kick.

Back Kick

Illus. 119 (below). In a horse stance or ready stance, bring your right leg up with the knee high in front of you.

Illus. 120 (right). With a driving force, kick straight behind you, locking the leg.

Illus. 121 (below right). Return your leg to the original stance. Always turn your head behind you to check the striking area.

Roundhouse Kick

The roundhouse kick will show you the results of your hard training by the way you increase your speed.

Illus. 122 (left). Move into a left front stance, and lift your right leg straight up. Drop your knee downwards and to your left while keeping your hand in front of you.

Illus. 123 (below left). From this position and angle, snap your leg completely around. Use the ball of the foot to strike.

Illus. 124 (below). Snap the kick back immediately to the original position, placing your foot back into the front stance. Practise with your left leg also.

Front Snap Kick

Illus. 125 (below). To throw the snap kick, stand in a left front stance with both hands guarding your body. Lift your right leg, bringing the knee towards your chest.

Illus. 126 (right). Hold your knee still and watch your balance as you snap the foot out with your toes back to kick.

Illus. 127 (below right). Strike with the ball of the foot. Snap back quickly, and return to a left front stance.

Front Jump Kick

Use the front jump kick to gain extra power to your kick and to get a greater reach in height for contact.

Illus. 128 (left). Move into a left front stance. Jump by shifting your weight to your front leg. Bring your right knee up high.

Illus. 129 (below left). While in the air, snap out your left leg into a front thrust kick.

Illus. 130 (below). Land on your right leg first; then your left leg to complete the kick.

Spinning-Blade Kick

Use the spinning-blade kick against a larger opponent.

Illus. 131 (right). Stand in a left back stance. Jump into the air off your left leg and spin your body completely around. Keep your right leg high.

Illus. 132 (below). Spin in the air.

Illus. 133 (below right). Lock your right leg straight out, and land on your left leg. This kick can also be done without the jump, by standing on your left leg and rotating on the ground.

Crescent Kick

Use the crescent kick to block a punch or to strike.

Illus. 134 (left). Move into a left front stance.

Illus. 135 (below left). Bring the right leg up behind you and to your side.

Illus. 136 (below). Kick your leg across in front of your body; then continue to move your right leg inward towards your left knee to complete the kick.

Stomping Kick

An excellent kick to master and easy to execute.

Illus. 137 (right). From a ready stance, lift your right leg straight up above your head.

Illus. 138 (left). Slam the kick downward using the heel.

4
KUMITE

Huehnergarth

Illus. 139. In kumite, or free-style sparring, you have no idea what your opponent will do.

Situations change because you and your opponent are both trying to score points with kicks, punches, and strikes. Since each opponent is a moving target, your position and timing are important. You must learn to kick and punch where you think your opponent will be moving.

You and a friend can kumite in a tournament, or in a gym or garage. But *be careful*. In many tournaments, especially at the lower ranks, you do not make contact. You simply need to strike within one or two inches of the target areas without being blocked.

INFRACTIONS

When sparring you must be careful not to violate a rule or get an infraction. If a judge raises his hand in a circular manner, this means a rule has been broken. An infraction can occur if you strike your opponent too low—usually below the belt. Going out of the ring or demonstrating poor sportsmanship can also result in an infraction, as can striking or charging at your opponent. If you are charged with an infraction, you could receive a warning, lose a point, or be disqualified. It depends upon whether the infraction is repeated or anger was shown. It is important to be extra careful and always be a good sportsman.

RULES

Illus. 140. When you enter a tournament you must have a gi, as well as hand and foot gloves. Some tournaments require head gear for extra protection.

Illus. 141. You can also wear additional equipment to protect your arms and legs.

You kumite with opponents of the same rank. You are also matched by size, and should be matched with an opponent of similar age. Rank is the most important factor in skill matching, but age and size are also considered for safety reasons.

STARTING THE MATCH

Illus. 142. In most kumite matches, there are a center judge and two corner judges.

Illus. 143. Always bow at the beginning of the match to show respect. Bow first to the center judge, then to your opponent.

When you make a clear strike or kick which is not blocked, you are awarded a point (some tournaments award two points for a kick). If you are blocked, no point is awarded. Since two of the three judges must agree on the score, you sometimes may strike successfully, but find that two judges did not see the point.

However, it is important never to argue with judges about their decisions. Let the judges and tournament officials work out any problems and always respect their decisions.

If you score the first three points or have the most points, you win the match. In case of a tie, the match continues until the first point is scored.

Do your best. Tournament fighting is rough, and the speed is fast, but with the proper preparation you will be successful. Remember to be careful, and not to hit—just come close.

OFFENSIVE TECHNIQUES

Situation 1

Illus. 145. Face your opponent in a front stance. Quickly execute a snap kick to the stomach to score.

Situation 2

Illus. 146. From a horse stance, move quickly and score a side kick to your opponent.

Situation 3

Illus. 147. While in a front stance, use your front (lead) leg to score with a quick roundhouse kick.

Situation 4

Illus. 148. In a front stance, move into a power roundhouse kick with your back leg.

Situation 5

Illus. 149. Facing your opponent in a front stance, you deliver a front kick. It is blocked.

Illus. 150. To score, immediately deliver a reverse punch to your opponent's body.

Situation 6

Illus. 151. You back into a horse stance, and try to score with a side kick. However, your opponent blocks the kick.

Illus. 152. To score, deliver a back fist to your opponent's head.

Situation 7

Illus. 153. From a front stance, deliver a quick roundhouse kick. It is immediately blocked.

Illus. 154. Score quickly with a reverse punch.

Situation 8

Illus. 155. Move into a front stance. Deliver a power roundhouse, which is blocked.

Illus. 156. In a quick and un-expected response, strike out with a front kick for the point.

Situation 9

Illus. 157. In a horse stance, deliver a side kick, which is blocked.

Illus. 158. Your back fist is also blocked.

Illus. 159. Score with a front kick from a front stance.

Illus. 160. Throw a back fist to move your opponent back.

Illus. 161. With a quick surprise for your opponent, deliver a spinning back kick to your opponent's stomach for the score.

DEFENSE SITUATION

In these situations, you must block your opponent's first strike and score with a fast technique.

Situation 1

Illus. 162. You block your opponent's front kick with a lower block.

Illus. 163. Deliver a front punch for the point.

Illus. 164. Block a side kick with a lower block.

Illus. 165. Step in fast and score with a back fist to your opponent's head.

80

Situation 3

Illus. 166. Block your opponent's roundhouse kick to your head with a rising block.

Illus. 167. Deliver a front kick to your opponent's stomach for the point.

81

Situation 4

Illus. 168. In this situation, your opponent comes quickly with a back fist to your head. Quickly block the back fist with a shuto block.

Illus. 169. Spot the opening on your opponent, and deliver a fast side kick for the point.

Situation 5

Illus. 170. You block a fast reverse punch to your chest area with an inside center block.

Illus. 171. Deliver a ridge hand strike to your opponent's head.

Situation 6

Illus. 172. Block your opponent's punch with a crescent kick.

Illus. 173. Immediately drive a back fist to catch your opponent off guard and score.

Illus. 174. Your opponent delivers a side kick. Block the kick with a lower block.

Illus. 175. Block the back fist with a shuto block and score with a reverse punch.

Situation 8

Illus. 176. Your opponent is extremely fast. Block him with a crescent kick.

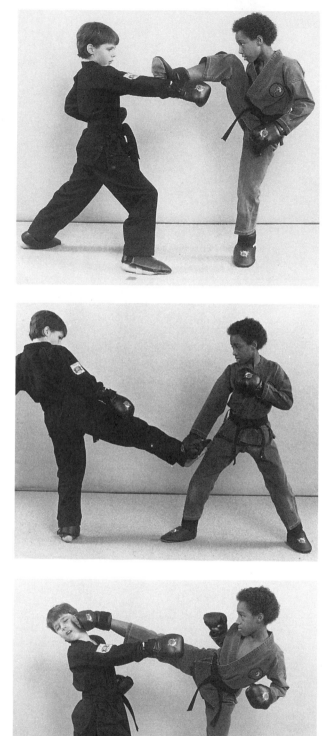

Illus. 177. Block the quick front kick.

Illus. 178. Sidestep and throw a roundhouse kick to score.

Situation 9

Illus. 179. Here comes your opponent with a lunge punch. Quickly block with a crescent kick.

Illus. 180. Score with a punch.

Situation 10

Illus. 181. Your opponent comes fast with a jumping front kick.

Illus. 182. Sidestep and cover your body area. At the same time, throw a fast front kick for the score.

88

FAKES

Experienced kumite fighters use a variety of techniques for scoring, including speed and strong desire. However, the ultimate winners also incorporate fakes into their fighting skills.

Situation 1

Illus. 183. From a front stance, pretend to deliver a front kick.

Illus. 184. Just as you begin to extend the front kick, quickly shift and deliver a round-house kick.

Illus. 185. In a horse stance, begin to extend a back fist.

Illus. 186. As soon as your opponent begins to block the back fist, skip and deliver a swift side kick to score.

90

Illus. 187. From a front stance, fake a back fist.

Illus. 188. As your opponent begins to block, deliver a ridge-hand strike to the head.

Situation 4

Illus. 189. While in a back stance, fake a roundhouse kick to your opponent's head.

Illus. 190. As your opponent begins to block, immediately drop your leg and shift your front leg into a quick roundhouse kick to your opponent's stomach or head.

Situation 5

Illus. 191. This is for the more flashy fighter. Catch your opponent off guard by faking a front punch.

Illus. 192. As the opponent moves and blocks, shift into a spinning heel kick. Be careful!

SELF DEFENSE

Some tournaments have self-defense events, either as competition or as demonstrations. These self-defense techniques can be used for demonstration or for your own protection.

Situation 1

Illus. 193. You are grabbed from behind in a choke hold.

Illus. 194. Lower your chin into the inside elbow joint so that you can breathe.

Illus. 195. Rotate your body inward towards your opponent and pull your head out. Hold onto your opponent's arm for a break.

Illus. 196. After the break, deliver a front kick to your opponent's ribs.

Situation 2

Illus. 197. Use a shuto against a strike.

Illus. 198. Strike your opponent with a palm-heel strike.

Illus. 199. Follow with a back fist.

Illus. 200. Finish with a front kick.

Situation 3

Illus. 201. Block a punch with a rising block.

Illus. 202. Grab and deliver an arm break.

Illus. 203. Hold onto the arm and rotate further.

Illus. 204. Finish with a driving-down arm break. These severe techniques would *only* be used if your life were in danger.

WINNING KUMITE

Strive to develop your own style. Know your power and speed, and learn to use your strengths. For example, you may develop a super-fast roundhouse kick or a powerful side kick. Work these into your sparring.

Know your distance. Learn to use your reach and know it without thinking. The difference of a few inches may mean a score or a "no point."

Learn your weaknesses, such as dropping your head and leaning forward. This can make your head an easy target. Identify and improve your weaknesses through dedication and practice.

5
KATAS

Illus. 205. Katas are planned moves that look like ballet or dance. You can use katas to practise your blocks, kicks, strikes, and punches in a graceful pattern of movements.

Most advanced katas look like the movements of animals, such as cats, snakes, or tigers; or like letters of the alphabet, such as H, T, K, or a plus sign (+).

Many instructors use katas that were developed by the great karate masters. Instructors change some katas or create new ones to help their students.

Practise each kata step in order. As you improve your skills, you can learn katas that are more difficult.

KATA COMPETITION

Kata competitions allow you to demonstrate a prearranged set of kicks, punches, and blocks that show your karate ability.

All katas have names. They are either known by their English names, such as "The Breathing Dragon" or "Crane on a Rock," or Japanese names, such as *Heian* (he-ON).

After you complete your kata, you will be given a score from one to ten, with ten being the highest. To avoid ties, some tournaments use a decimal system such as 4.2, 3.6, etc.

After you perform your kata, you receive a score from each judge. The highest total score wins. Awards are given for first, second, and third place.

The way you breathe when you perform is very important. Keep a lot of air in your lungs. Take a deep breath before you do a block, kick, or a strike. Exhale as you do the movement. Breathing out heavily when doing the final action in a series will increase your strength. Shout a loud "ee-ay" while breathing out. This will improve your power and confidence. But do it only in the last move in a series.

Sheno Kata

Illus. 207. Begin with a bow; then breathe in as you bend your left leg and cross your arms in front of you.

Illus. 208. Breathe out and stand in a ready stance.

Illus. 209. Step forward into a left front stance and do a left low block.

Illus. 210. Do a right front kick and return to a left front stance.

Illus. 211. Punch at chest level with your right fist.

Illus. 212. Follow with a left punch.

Illus. 213. Turn your head to your left; then turn your body to your left as well. Stay in a left front stance and do a rising block with your left arm.

Illus. 214. Do a front kick with your right foot at stomach level and return your foot to the floor.

Illus. 215. Throw a right punch.

Illus. 216. Follow with a left punch.

Illus. 217. Pivot on your left leg, turning 180° around to your right side into a right front stance.

Illus. 218. At the same time, do an inside middle block with your right arm.

Illus. 219. Do a left front kick to the stomach area.

Illus. 220. Return your foot and throw a left punch to the head area.

Illus. 221. Follow with a right punch to the lower body area. Shout "ee-ay" as you do the punch.

Illus. 222. Turn your right leg 90° to your right into a right front stance and do a closed "X" block. Your back is now to the judges.

Illus. 223. Throw a left front kick. Do an inside middle block with your right arm.

Illus. 224. Without moving either foot, do an inside middle block with your left arm.

Illus. 225. Punch to the chest area with your right fist.

Illus. 226. Follow with a left punch.

Illus. 227. Now, another right punch.

Illus. 228. Lift your left leg and spin completely around to the left towards your original position, facing the judges.

Illus. 229. Breathe in and cross your arms in front of you.

Illus. 230. Breathe out and lower your arms and right leg. Close your stance and bow.

Heian Two

This kata is typical of the Heian series, though it is slightly more advanced. For Heian One, see *Karate to Win* (Sterling, 1987).

Illus. 231 (below). Move into a right back stance and execute a left inside middle block and a right rising block at the same time.

Illus. 232 (right). Drop your left arm and strike with a right upside-down punch.

Illus. 233 (below right). Step into a horse stance and strike out with a left fist.

Illus. 234 (above). Move into a left back stance with a right inside middle block and left rising block.

Illus. 235 (above right). Drop your right arm and strike with a left upside-down punch.

Illus. 236 (right). Step into a horse stance and strike out with a right fist.

Illus. 237 (left). Pull up to the right foot into a closed stance. Pull your left fist over your right hand, and look behind you. Deliver a right side kick with a right fist.

Illus. 238 (below left). Move into a right back stance and execute a left knife-hand strike.

Illus. 239 (below). Step up and deliver a right knife-hand strike from a left back stance.

Illus. 240 (above left). Move up again into a right back stance and deliver a left knife-hand strike.

Illus. 241 (above). Push your left hand down, and move into a right front stance and deliver a spear hand.

Illus. 242 (left). Turn to the left by bringing your right leg far behind your body.

Illus. 243 (above). Continue around and deliver a knife-hand strike with your left hand from a right back stance.

Illus. 244 (above right). Step out to the left at a 45° angle in a left back stance while striking with a right knife-hand strike.

Illus. 245 (right). Swing your body to the right and place your left knife hand in front. Draw your right hand, palm inward, to your left ear.

Illus. 246 (left). Deliver a right knife-hand strike, straight ahead, in a left back stance.

Illus. 247 (below left). Place your left foot close to your right and bring your left hand, palm inward, to your right ear. Deliver a left knife-hand strike 45° to the right in a right back stance.

Illus. 248 (below). Move your left foot into a left front stance. Your back is to the judges. Block an imaginary kick with a right inside block.

Illus. 249 (below). Immediately throw a right front kick.

Illus. 250 (right). Move into a right front stance and deliver a left front punch.

Illus. 251 (below right). Immediately block with a left inside block in the same stance.

Illus. 252 (below). Deliver a left front kick.

Illus. 253 (right). Punch with a right fist.

Illus. 254 (below right). Step up into a right front stance and swing both arms into a block. The swing gives you extra strength.

Illus. 255 (left). Spin around as into a left front stance.

Illus. 256 (below left). Deliver a left lower block.

Illus. 257 (below). Lean back slightly and block upwards with a left shuto block.

Illus. 258 (left). Pretend to grab the blocked arm. Step 45° to your right into a rising right arm block.

Illus. 259 (below left). Turn into a right front stance and deliver a right lower block.

Illus. 260 (below). Lean back slightly and block upwards with a right shuto block.

Illus. 261. Cup the blocked arm and step into a 45° rising left arm block.

Illus. 262. Step the left leg back into a closed stance and bow.

127

INDEX